The Story of
ZHUANGZI

www.royalcollins.com

Picture Story Book of Ancient Chinese Thinkers

The Story of ZHUANGZI

Zhao Mingjun

Translated by Wu Meilian

Books Beyond Boundaries

ROYAL COLLINS

Picture Story Books of Ancient Chinese Thinkers
The Story of ZHUANGZI

Zhao Mingjun
Translated by Wu Meilian

First published in 2024 by Royal Collins Publishing Group Inc.
Groupe Publication Royal Collins Inc.
550-555 boul. René-Lévesque O Montréal (Québec) H2Z1B1 Canada

ISBN: 979-8-9852490-6-4

To find out more about our publications, please visit www.royalcollins.com.

In Zhuangzi's rich and romantic spiritual world, one can transform with butterflies, engage in dialogue with ghosts and spirits, and comprehend philosophy from bizarre and fantastical scenes.

From Zhuangzi's daily life to his words and deeds, through exaggerated yet humorous depictions, and in the elegant and ethereal artistic conception of ink-wash painting, this book guides us on a "fantastical" journey to the world of Zhuangzi.

Zhuangzi's surname was Zhou. His birth and death years, family background, and the origins of his teachers have always been historical mysteries. Based on the records of *Zhuangzi*, *Records of the Grand Historian*, and other ancient texts, it is speculated that Zhuangzi was born in the State of Song in the middle of the Warring States Period (475–221 BCE), a contemporary of King Hui of the State of Wei and King Xuan of the State of Qi.

Zhuangzi, also known as *Nanhua Jing*, is one of the Daoist classics, a collection of works by Zhuangzi and his later disciples. It is highly valued in the research of both philosophy and literature.

During the Warring States Period, vassal states fought endlessly for power and land, and various schools of thought competed for rulers' favor. Among the many thinkers, Zhuangzi stood alone. Like a reclusive hermit, he dreamed of changing into a butterfly and flying freely around. After he woke up, he wondered whether he had dreamed of becoming a butterfly or whether the butterfly had changed into Zhuangzi at that moment.

In the book *Zhuangzi*, there is a giant bird, Peng, that can soar in the sky 28,000 miles high, and short-sighted small birds that ridicule his achievement. There are battles constantly taking place between two countries living on a snail's two tentacles and a black Chinese dragon guarding a precious pearl under the sea. The visitors to Zhuangzi's dreams were not only butterflies but also talking skeletons.

One day, on his way to the State of Chu, Zhuangzi saw a skull by the side of the road, so he bowed to it and asked, "What crime did you commit? What disaster did you suffer? Why are you in such a pitiable state now?" The skull did not answer. Zhuangzi pulled it over and fell asleep with his head resting on top of it.

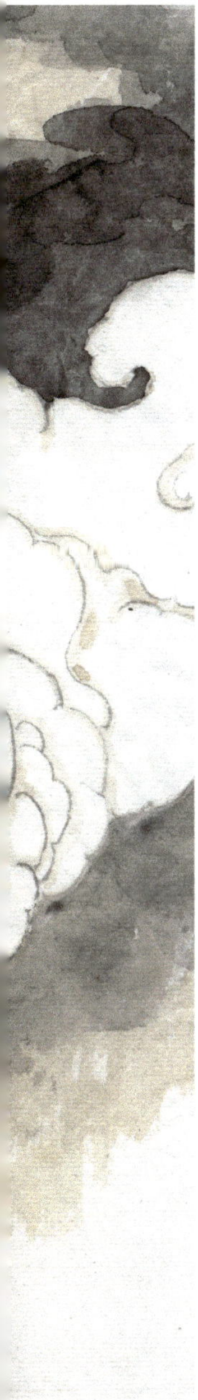

That night, the skull visited Zhuangzi in his dreams and said, "Sir, you seem to be eloquent. You know the worries of life, such as hunger, illness, and pain, but how much do you know about death? The human world is full of burdens and suffering, and life itself is a toil. But in the world after death, there are no fatuous kings, no bullying officials, and no changing of the seasons. Heaven and Earth are the masters of all. I have finally made an eternal farewell to the troubles of life and will not exchange my freedom and joy of this moment even if you offer me to sit on the throne."

Zhuangzi, who fully understood the ways of nature and the human world, was not very particular about material life. Once, he had an audience with King Wei of the State of Hui wearing patched, ragged clothes and a pair of old shoes tied with hemp rope. King Hui asked him why he looked so poor and in despair, and Zhuangzi replied, "Wearing rags and shoes is poverty; having ideals but not being able to implement them is in despair."

King Wei of the State of Chu admired Zhuangzi's talent and wanted to appoint him to be Prime Minister. His messenger found Zhuangzi fishing by the Pu River. Zhuangzi said to him without looking back, "A thousand-year-old turtle would rather crawl and drag its tail in the mud than offer its shell to be worshiped in a human temple." In Zhuangzi's view, becoming an official in the court is tantamount to being a sacrificial ox covered in brocade and enjoying fine grass and grains. But when the time comes for it to be slaughtered in the Ancestral Temple, it will be too late for it to wish to go back to its old, carefree days.

Although Zhuangzi had no intention of becoming an official, other people still got jealous and slanderous. After his friend Hui Shi (Huizi)* became the Prime Minister of the State of Wei, Zhuangzi planned to visit him. Someone told Huizi that Zhuangzi was here to compete for his position, so Huizi ordered a search for Zhuangzi in the city for three days and three nights.

Zhuangzi heard about it and came to see Huizi himself. He said, "There is a bird in the south called *yuanchu*. It flies from the South Sea to the North Sea, only rests on the tall sycamore tree, eats bamboo, and drinks sweet and pure spring water. There is an owl that only eats stinky rotten mice and thinks that the *yuanchu* will steal its food, so it makes a threatening sound to scare the *yuanchu* off. Now, are you trying to scare me off with your stinky rotten mouse?"

* Hui Shi was from the State of Song. He was a famous politician and founder of the School of Names.

漆園

Zhuangzi laughed off his friend's misunderstanding, and he responded to the worldly snobbery with biting sarcasm. According to the *Records of the Grand Historian*, Zhuangzi once served as a gardening official, but he did not serve long due to his aloofness and noble character.

He lived in a shabby house and supported himself by weaving sandals, sometimes too poor to eat. One day, he had no choice but to borrow some grains from an official supervising the river course. The official said, “I will soon receive money from my fiefdom; how about I lend you 300 taels of gold by then?”

Zhuangzi’s well
Located in Qingliansi Village, Minquan County, Shangqiu City, Henan Province. It is said that Zhuangzi had drawn water from it.

Zhuangzi answered, "On my way here, I met a fish calling for help in a rut that was about to dry up. It said it came from the East Sea and asked me for a bowl of water so it could survive. I promised him that I would go talk to the Kings of the states of Wu and Yue and build a canal to bring all the water from the Xijiang River to save it. The fish was very upset and said, 'I have lost my home and only asked for a bowl of water to live. If you wish to go thousands of miles to look for water, you may better look for me at the fish market!' "

There was a powerful villain in the State of Song called Cao Shang. He received one hundred carriages as a reward from the King of Qin after a mission to Qin. When he saw Zhuangzi, he laughed at his poverty. "Mr. Zhuang," he said, "I'm not as good as you in living in shabby alleys and starving, but I dare say you are not as good as me when it comes to pleasing the King of Qin and receiving huge rewards!"

Zhuangzi did not defend himself. He simply replied, "I hear that the King of Qin is ill. He awards people who cure his abscess with one carriage and anyone who cures his hemorrhoids by licking five carriages. The humbler the treatment, the bigger the awards. Judging from the hundred carriages you received, I suppose you have cured all his hemorrhoids."

King Wen of the State of Zhao was fond of swordsmanship, and swordsmen came to demonstrate their skills one after another, fighting each other and causing many casualties. As the fervor for sword fighting led to an increasing number of idlers, the power of the State of Zhao gradually declined. The prince was worried about this, so he asked Zhuangzi for advice, with a thousand taels of gold as a reward. Zhuangzi accepted the request but refused the gold. He approached King Wen in the attire of a swordsman and said, without bowing, "My swords can kill anyone within ten steps. I can walk with them for thousands of miles, and no one will be able to stop me."

King Wen was very happy to hear this, "Your swordsmanship is really invincible in the world!" He thus called the best swordsmen in the country to compete with Zhuangzi. Zhuangzi was not in a hurry to go upstage them.

Instead, he said to the king, "I have three swords, and Your Majesty may pick one. The first is the King's Sword, with Mount Shicheng of Yanxi and Mount Tai of Qi as its blades, the States of Jin and Wei as its body, the direct ruling region of Zhou and the State of Song as its rings, and the States of Han and Wei as its handle. The King's Sword is wrapped with the four realms outside the Central Plains, surrounded by the four seasons, and protected by the Bohai Sea and the Hengshan Mountain. The owner of the King's Sword can create a new world with invincible force and make everyone surrender to him.

The second is the Feudal Lord's Sword, with the wise, brave, and honest people as its blades, the virtuous people as its body, the loyal people as its rings, and the heroic people as its handles. The owner of the Feudal Lord's Sword can make all subjects in the world obey the orders of the monarch.

The third is the Commoner's Sword. The people who use this sword have messy hair and red eyes. They fight with their lives but are of no use to the world. Your Majesty, you are in the position of the king, but you like to use the Commoner's Sword."

After that day, King Wen gave up on this violent hobby and devoted himself to state affairs.

Prime Minister Dang of the State of Song asked Zhuangzi about benevolence, and Zhuangzi replied, “Tigers and wolves also have benevolence.” Zhuangzi is more willing to believe that compared with humans, wild animals that look ferocious but never pretend to cover their nature have the benevolence of loving each other.

Prime Minister Dang asked again, “What is the highest benevolence?”

Zhuangzi replied, “The highest benevolence is to have no difference when treating the intimate and the distant.” Ordinary benevolence means treating others the way one wishes to be treated, but Zhuangzi’s benevolence is giving up self-centeredness.

In the era in which Zhuangzi lived, scholars of all schools of thought were keen to promote their theories as the best for the world. Zhuangzi watched them argue and lamented the loss of true Way in the endless debates. He expressed his comment through this story, "Once upon a time, there was an old man who raised monkeys. When he was giving out acorn chestnuts to the monkeys, he offered the monkeys three chestnuts in the morning and four in the evening, but the monkeys were angry about the plan. He then offered them four in the morning and three in the evening, and the monkeys were happy again. They did not know that the sum of three and four had never changed."

In Zhuangzi's view, superficial contradictions such as right and wrong, beauty and ugliness, kindness and evil are all included in the Great Way. People create divisions and endless debates that exhaust their minds. This is no different from getting happy or upset about chestnuts like the monkeys.

The allusion of "Sinking Fish and Falling Geese" came from "Equality of Things." It is often used to describe the stunning beauty of women. But the original meaning in *Zhuangzi* is, "Beauty in people's eyes is nothing to animals. The beautiful Mao Qiang and Lady Li, when the fish see them, they dive into the bottom of the water, the birds fly high into the sky, and the elk run away quickly. They don't know people's beauty and ugliness, simply fleeing because of fear." Why should people speculate on the feelings of other beings based on their own invented definition of beauty?

People living in wetlands will suffer from backaches and diseases, but fish will not; people living in trees will be afraid, but apes will not. Zhuangzi explains that there is no yardstick to follow with the definitions of benevolence, righteousness, and truth that debaters all over the world have been arguing about, because the standards vary from person to person.

Lady Li was the daughter of King Lirong. When she first came to the Jin Palace, she suffered from homesickness and uncertainty about the future, and she cried all day. But after she got the favor of Duke Xian of the State of Jin, she enjoyed all kinds of luxuries in life, and she regretted the tears she had shed for her past ignorance. In Zhuangzi's opinion, people may also regret worrying about death in their lives after they have experienced it.

To Zhuangzi, life and death are just different states of life, like the two aspects of right and wrong, kindness and evil, and beauty and ugliness, neither of which is absolute. Therefore, there is no need to be overly sad or happy about them.

When Zhuangzi's wife passed away, his good friend Huizi came to express his condolences. He found Zhuangzi sitting in the mourning hall with his legs spread apart, knocking on a basin and singing, as if his wife's death had nothing to do with him. This seemingly bizarre story of "Singing Knocking on the Basin" best embodies Zhuangzi's optimism and detachment toward the changes of life and death.

Zhuangzi's attitude shocked Huizi, who asked, "You and your wife have lived together for so many years. She raised your children, took care of the housework, and lived with you in poverty. Now that she is dead, not only can you not shed one tear for her, but you even sing in front of her coffin. Isn't that too despicable?"

Zhuangzi replied, "How could I really be indifferent toward her death and not cry when she first left me? But was I not alone before she was born? Did her form and soul not exist before she came to the world? All lives, including hers and mine, change from "not being" to "being," with concrete forms and existences created by vague, chaotic breaths before changing back to the pure and peaceful "not being" through death. If you see it this way, the changes in human lives are like the changes in seasons. When my beloved returns her life calmly to the universe, why do I have to shed unnecessary tears?"

One day, Zhuangzi and Huizi at Haoshui River. They stood on a bridge and watched the little fish swimming below. "The fish are so happy!" said Zhuangzi admiringly. Huizi asked, "You are not a fish; how do you know that the fish are happy?" Zhuangzi wanted to tease his old friend, so he also answered with a question, "You are not me. How do you know that I don't know that the fish are happy?"

Huizi persisted, "I am not you, and I don't know if you know that the fish are happy or not. But you are also not a fish, so how do you know if the fish are happy?" Zhuangzi smiled, "Well, I know it from this bridge!" Then, he went back to watching the fish again.

Huizi criticized Zhuangzi's remarks as absurd and useless, like a gourd too big to be made into cups or a tree of heaven with tangled roots that cannot be used by carpenters. However, Zhuangzi believed that the same thing could have very different effects when used in different places. People should explore the maximum value of things to make perfect use of them. His own teachings were of great use, but Huizi could not fully understand them.

He told Huizi a story, "There was a family in Song who made chilblain medicine, and they have made their livings by rinsing silk for generations. One day, a man came from afar and offered a hundred taels of gold for their recipe. Then, he used this medicine to help the State of Wu defeat the State of Yue in a water battle in winter. He received a huge reward and fiefdom from the King of Wu."

“Some people used the chilblain medicine to rinse silk, while others used it to win wars and awards. Why not change the big gourd into a boat and float around the world? The tree of heaven may be useless to carpenters, but it can protect itself from being cut down and provide people with shade to rest.”

People all know the value of being useful, but few understand the value of being useless. Zhuangzi believed that "the usefulness of uselessness" is most valuable. However, he was also aware of the exceptions in life. He had seen big trees escape the fate of being cut down because of their poor material quality, but poultry were slaughtered earlier because they could not crow. Sometimes, those who were useful could not enjoy their life to the full, but sometimes, those who were useless could not escape an early death either. Faced with the unpredictable future and the ubiquitous dilemmas in life, Zhuangzi said, "Let's place ourselves between usefulness and uselessness, although this may not be perfect."

Huizi prided himself on his eloquence throughout his life, and he especially liked to argue with Zhuangzi about right and wrong. Although they often had different views, their debates were full of witty remarks, and their relationship was quite extraordinary.

After Huizi's death, Zhuangzi visited his grave. He did not cry but told a story, "A painter in the capital of Chu got a piece of white paint the size of a fly's wing on the tip of his nose, and he asked a nearby craftsman named Shi to help him remove it. Craftsman Shi picked up an ax and swung it at him without even looking. There was a whistling sound of wind, and the white paint disappeared in an instant, while the painter's nose was unhurt. Lord Songyuan heard this strange news and sent the craftsman Shi to the palace to perform his trick on himself. The craftsman said sadly: 'I used to be able to swing an ax like that, but the person who could do the trick with luck with me had long passed away . . .' "

After telling the story, Zhuangzi looked at Huizi's tombstone and said, "Since you died, there is no one I can talk to anymore. I don't know what I can say now." The pain of losing a close friend in the cold, vast world is beyond expression.

Zhuangzi especially liked to use fables to express his thoughts. In the fable "Cook Ding Dismembers the Ox," he said, "The Cook Ding has extraordinary skills with killing an ox. He knows the animal's body well, and he can easily find and move his knife through the gaps between the ox's tendons and bones so that the ox's body can be divided into parts like scattered chunks. The whole process of the slaughtering is natural and smooth, which is pleasing to the eyes of the onlookers. An ordinary chef chops the bones of the ox directly, and he has to change his knife every month; a good chef chops the muscles and tendons, and he changes his knife once a year. Cook Ding, however, has been using the same knife for nineteen years to slaughter thousands of oxen, but the blade of the knife is still sharp and like new. The key lies in his ability to 'do it at ease.' "*

Practice makes perfect, but Zhuangzi's emphasis was not on superficial skills. He admired the ability to follow the law of nature in things to achieve perfection, which is close to the Way itself.

---

* "Do it with ease": The knife moves freely between the tendons and bones of the ox without hindrance. This idiom is later used to describe doing things skillfully and easily.

In *Zhuangzi*, there are some weird-looking but enlightened characters. In "The Great Master," a man named Ziyu is so sick that his back is hunched, his internal organs are displaced, and his cheeks close to his navel. Nevertheless, he still walked with difficulty to the well, admired his own reflection, and praised the Creator for turning him into a composer. He said, "If the Creator turns my left arm into a rooster, I will use it to announce the dawn; if the Creator turns my right arm into a slingshot, I will use it to shoot owls for my barbecue; if the Creator turns my tailbone turned into a wheel and my spirit into a horse, I will ride it and travel around!"

In Zhuangzi's view, the physical body's completeness and beauty are not important as long as the inner virtue of the person is high. Zhuangzi also advocated that people should be at ease with the times and accept all changes in appearance given by nature.

Once, Zhuangzi went to a chestnut forest at Diaoling. An unusually large bird came from the south, with wings seven *chi* wide and eyes one *cun* big.* Zhuangzi picked up his bow and followed quickly, preparing to shoot this strange bird.

---

* Both *chi* and *cun* are ancient Chinese length units. Seven *chi* equals about 91 inches, and one *cun* equals about 1.3 inches.

Just then, Zhuangzi saw a cicada resting alone in the shade of a tree, not aware of a mantis behind him, ready to catch it. The mantis, however, also did not know that the big bird had landed behind it, waiting for an opportunity to hunt. Seeing this, Zhuangzi realized that all things in the world were intertwined and interacted with each other, so he dropped his bow and ran away. The gardener, however, thought he was a thief and cursed him. Zhuangzi returned home and kept thinking about this experience for a long time.

His disciple Linju asked him what was bothering him, and Zhuangzi told him the story that "the mantis stalks the cicada, but the oriole is at its back." He said, "I used to only know how to preserve the body in stillness, but I forgot about myself in movement. I can see the dangers that people are in when they chase fame and wealth, but I don't know how to avoid it myself. I have lost my true nature and got myself in trouble when I was obsessed with the external objects, just like those praying mantises and orioles."

While other thinkers tried their best to promote their own theories, Zhuangzi never regarded his words and deeds as rules and models for the world. He frankly reflected on his observations and confusion. As he put his thoughts into words, he reflected on the meaning of the verbal expressions as well. In his view, language certainly has its value, but the best meaning in the world is often beyond words. People cherish books but often miss the more important, implied meaning that's not written.

The importance of "implied meaning" can be seen in the fable "Lunbian Cuts a Wheel." One day, Duke Huan of Qi was reading ancient texts in the palace hall, and a craftsman, Lunbian, was cutting wood and making wheels below the steps. Lunbian said to Duke Huan, "Since the saints who wrote the books are dead, what you are reading is just the dross left by the sages!"

Duke Huan said angrily, “How can you, a craftsman who makes wheels, talk about the books of sages? If you can’t explain yourself, I will sentence you to death!” Lunbian answered, “I know this from my own experience. I know the secret of cutting wheels, but I can’t express it through words. I am seventy years old now, and I can only cut wheels by myself, because I cannot even teach my son to do it.”

"The ancient sages who wrote the book had died, and they took their thoughts that could not be written with them. Of course, what you read can only be the dross left behind." Duke Huan was very impressed, and he spared Lunbian.

When Zhuangzi came to the end of his life, his disciples wished to give him a rich burial, but Zhuangzi refused. He said, "Let Heaven and Earth be my coffin and the sun and the moon be its decoration, let the stars be my burial jewels and the birds and animals be my sacrifices. Isn't that rich enough?"

Zhuangzi followed the spontaneous course of nature throughout his life. He believed that although human lives are limited like fuel, their thoughts and spirits are like eternal flames that never die out. His own thoughts recorded in *Zhuangzi* are like such flames that continue to enlighten the world with brightness and heat from one generation to the next.

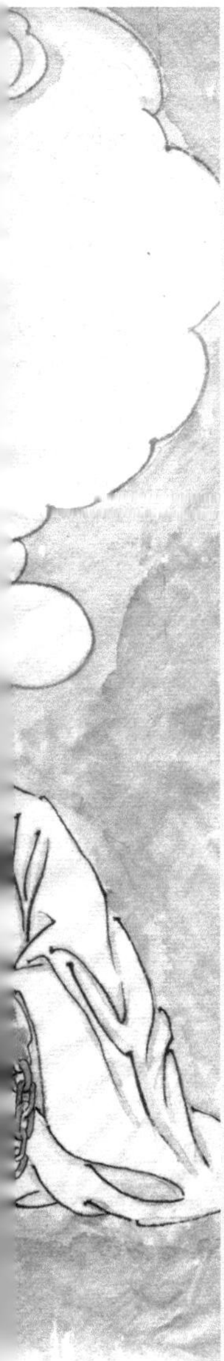

Zhuangzi's extraordinary wisdom and literary talent, his carefree spirit unfazed by glory and unbound by ethics, and his interesting, reclusive, and noble character have significantly influenced Sima Qian, Ruan Ji, Ji Kang, Tao Yuanming, Li Bai, and other literati in the later generations. The masterpiece *Zhuangzi* also had a profound impact on the metaphysical talks of the Wei and Jin dynasties, the pastoral literature or mythical works of the Southern and Northern Dynasties, the landscape poetry of the Tang Dynasty, and the novels and drama creations of the Ming and Qing dynasties. The magnificent colors that Zhuangzi's thoughts added to the Chinese civilization continue to shine through the depth of Chinese people's minds today.

ABOUT THE AUTHOR

Zhao Mingjun is a Chinese painting and comic strip artist. He has studied figure, bird, and flower painting under Zhou Tieheng, Zhao Mengzhu, Zhong Zhifu, and Yan Shaoxiang. His representative works include *The Battle of Bridge No. 7*, *A Backpack*, *The Red Seal*, *The Story of the Breakout of the Old City*, *Mineral Lamps*, *Capturing the Little Stovemaker Alive*, *Ming Shaocheng, the Fire-Fighting Hero*, and *Lian Jinfa, the Red Child.*